MALINKE

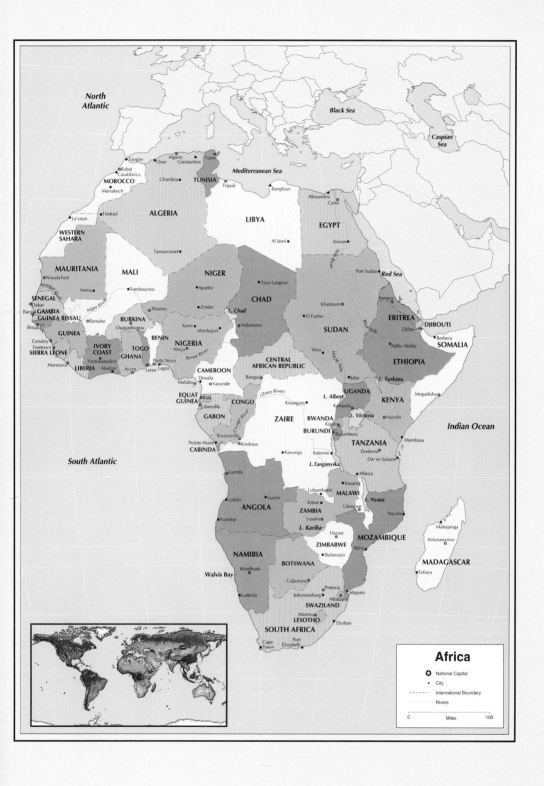

The Heritage Library of African Peoples

MALINKE

C. O. Nwanunobi, Ph.D.

THE ROSEN PUBLISHING GROUP, INC.
NEW YORK

FEB – – 1997

Published in 1996 by The Rosen Publishing Group, Inc.
29 East 21st Street, New York, NY 10010

Copyright 1996 by The Rosen Publishing Group, Inc.

First Edition

Manufactured in the United States of America

Library of Congress Cataloging-in-Publication Data

Nwanunobi, C. Onyeka.
    Malinke / C.O. Nwanunobi. — 1st ed.
        p.   cm. — (The heritage library of African peoples)
    Includes bibliographical references and index.
    Summary: Discusses the history, culture, religion, traditions, and daily life of the Malinke, West African people who live in the Manding Highlands near the upper Niger River.
    ISBN 0-8239-1979-X
    1. Mandingo (African people)—History—Juvenile literature.
2. Mandingo (African people)—Social life and customs—Juvenile literature. [1. Mandingo (African people)]   I. Title.
II. Series.
DT474.6.M36N85   1996
966.23′0049634—dc20   96-2218
                                                          CIP
                                                          AC

Contents

INTRODUCTION

THERE IS EVERY REASON FOR US TO KNOW
something about Africa and to understand its
past and the way of life of its peoples. Africa is a
rich continent that has for centuries provided
the world with art, culture, labor, wealth, and
natural resources. It has vast mineral deposits,
fossil fuels, and commercial crops.

But perhaps most important is the fact that
fossil evidence indicates that human beings
originated in Africa. The earliest traces of
human beings and their tools are almost two
million years old. Their descendants have
migrated throughout the world. To be human is
to be of African descent.

The experiences of the peoples who stayed in
Africa are as rich and as diverse as of those who
established themselves elsewhere. This series of
books describes their environment, their modes
of subsistence, their relationships, and their customs and beliefs. The books present the variety
of languages, histories, cultures, and religions
that are to be found on the African continent.
They demonstrate the historical linkages between
African peoples and the way contemporary Africa
has been affected by European colonial rule.

Africa is large, complex, and diverse. It en-
compasses an area of more than 11,700,000

square miles. The United States, Europe, and India could fit easily into it. The sheer size is an indication of the continent's great variety in geography, terrain, climate, flora, fauna, peoples, languages, and cultures.

Much of contemporary Africa has been shaped by European colonial rule, industrialization, urbanization, and the demands of a world economic system. For more than seventy years, large regions of Africa were ruled by Great Britain, France, Belgium, Portugal, and Spain. African peoples from various ethnic, linguistic, and cultural backgrounds were brought together to form colonial states.

For decades Africans struggled to gain their independence. It was not until after World War II that the colonial territories became independent African states. Today, almost all of Africa is ruled by Africans. Large numbers of Africans live in modern cities. Rural Africa is also being transformed, and yet its people still engage in many of their customs and beliefs.

Contemporary circumstances and natural events have not always been kind to ordinary Africans. Today, however, new popular social movements and technological innovations pose great promise for future development.

George C. Bond, Ph.D., Director
Institute of African Studies
Columbia University, New York

In Malinke societies, prominent families support *griots*, who are entertainers, storytellers, and recorders of oral history. This Malinke elder from the village of Kela, near the town of Kangaba in Mali, is from a leading family that supports several *griots*.

1

THE PEOPLE

THE MALINKE ARE ONE OF THE BEST-KNOWN peoples of the western portion of West Africa. They have large populations in the Republic of Guinea, Côte d'Ivoire (Ivory Coast), the Republic of Mali, Senegal, the Gambia, and Guinea Bissau. They also live in Liberia, Sierra Leone, Burkina Faso, and the northern parts of modern Ghana. In the 1300s Malinke culture stretched as far north as the southern edge of the Sahara Desert and southward to the Atlantic coast. From west to east it stretched from the upper reaches of the River Senegal to the country of the Hausa in present-day Nigeria.

The total Malinke population is now estimated at over five million. Their largest number is in the Republic of Guinea, followed by Côte d'Ivoire, Mali, and Senegal. The Malinke make up about half of the population of the Gambia.

The name Malinke comes from the Fulbe (Fulani) language. It means "the people of (the

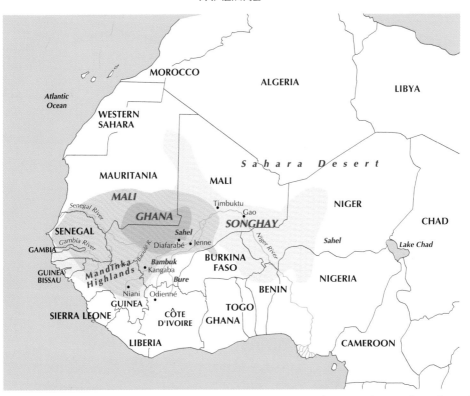

Today the Malinke are found in several countries of West Africa. They founded the Empire of Mali, which succeeded the Empire of Ghana and was in turn succeeded by the Songhay Empire. These three great empires are shaded in green on the map above. At its peak, the Empire of Mali extended east to Gao.

ancient empire of) Mali." They are also known as the Mandinka or Maninka. These are the names that the people themselves prefer. They are also called by the more popular name Mandingo. These last three names refer to the Malinke who live in the Manding Highlands near the upper Niger River. The Malinke are members of a much larger group of related peoples called the Mande.

The Malinke language is one of several West African languages found in the large Mande group. The Malinke language is the most widely used of all the Mande languages. High, medium, and low pitches are used to give different meanings to the same word. Such languages are described as tonal.

Malinke oral tradition describes their language as "clear." Modern linguists agree that it is a fairly easy language to learn. Because of its simplicity, and its relationship to several other languages in the region, it was quickly adopted by other people. It was one of the factors that helped unify the Mali Empire from the 1100s through the 1500s. Today, Malinke is the most widely used African language in the Gambia. It is still widely spoken in the Republic of Mali, Guinea, Guinea Bissau, and Senegal.

Part of the Empire of Mali was located within the state now known as the Republic of Mali. But the ancient Empire was different from the contemporary Republic in many ways. The Empire had lost most of its power by the early 1600s, three centuries before the modern republic was created. At the height of the Empire's power its territories extended to the Atlantic coast. In contrast today's Republic of Mali is landlocked. On the other hand, modern Mali extends into more northerly regions than did ancient Mali. Also, although the Malinke form a major group in the contemporary state of Mali, they do not dominate it as they did old Mali.

The few tall trees in the savanna are landmarks and resting places and often form the centers of villages where meetings and ceremonies are held in the shade. Seen here is the meeting place in the village of Kela in Mali. The raised platform is used for seating during important meetings.

In spite of these differences, some key areas of old Mali are still found within the modern republic. The Niger River, for example, has played an important role in the history, social, and economic life of both ancient Mali and modern Mali.

The name Republic of Mali was adopted by a group of West African people when they gained their independence from France in 1960. The name was chosen in recognition of the great achievements of the Empire of Mali in that part of Africa. It was a sign of respect that recalled this rich heritage. It also encouraged contemporary Malians to strive for similar greatness.▲

2

THE LAND

DURING THE TIME OF THE MALI EMPIRE, FROM 1240 to the early 1400s, Malinke territory lay in the savanna region of the western part of West Africa. The savanna extends from the southern edge of the Sahel to the northern borders of the forest zone near the coast of the Atlantic Ocean. In this region of West Africa, the savanna is mostly vast, open grassland. Malinke oral tradition speaks of their land as "The Bright Country." Trees are few, but those that thrive can attain great height and girth. These are mentioned in Malinke oral tradition as important landmarks. Also, they provide shade and serve as places for travelers to rest. Within villages, meetings and festive occasions are often organized around these trees.

The Malinke occupied mostly the middle and southern parts of the savanna. Their original

Part of the original home of the Malinke people was around the Baoulé River, seen here. This landscape in northwestern Côte d'Ivoire is typical of the savanna.

home was on the upper reaches of the Niger River and around its tributaries, the Sankarani and Baoulé Rivers. These rivers are important features of the environment, cutting through the land from the southwest to the northeast.

The Niger, the second-longest river in Africa, has always been the most reliable source of water for the region. Its banks and floodplains provide fertile fields for rice and other crops. Though obstructed by many falls and rapids, the Niger has always been a major route for communication among the peoples of this area. The Malinke refer to the Niger as Joliba and regard it with great respect.

For many centuries the Niger River has played an important role in the lives of Malinke people, who call it Joliba. Here the Sahara Desert stretches down to the vital water supply of the Niger River.

Malinke are noted for their farming. Their Fulani neighbors raise cattle and livestock. Malinke around the Niger also fish for food and for trade. Fishing rights for certain parts of the river may be shared between villages that fish in the same areas on different days. Fishing with a net is the most common method. Another interesting method is undertaken by the whole community: everyone works together to collect fish stranded on land when the Niger retreats. For those who migrated to areas west of the original home of the Malinke, the Senegal and Gambia Rivers and their tributaries were similarly important for farming and fishing.

Malinke oral tradition states that their land

Gold played a key role in the expansion of the Empire of Mali. Today Malinke villagers in Côte d'Ivoire still dig and pan for gold.

was originally made up of twelve provinces. These provinces formed the nucleus of the expanding Empire of Mali. The capital was Niani, very close to the River Sankarani. Niani was near the town of Bure, where gold was mined, and 625 miles southwest of the famous town of Timbuktu. Gold made Mali famous far beyond the continent of Africa. There were also large deposits of iron ore in the neighborhood. The area around Niani also supported a large population from which soldiers could be drafted. This contributed to Mali's strength. Moreover, the location could be easily defended.

The emperor of the Mali Empire and his courtiers lived in Niani, the center of culture and commerce. From Niani important trade routes extended to other parts of the empire and farther northeast to the Sahel and the Sahara. As the empire declined into the 1600s, Niani lost its importance and became a small town again. Today, it is remembered for its glorious history. It is still located within contemporary Mali, very near the Guinea border.

Very early in their history, the Malinke developed a culture of migration. Short-term migration occurs when there is little demand for labor on the farms and Malinke seek temporary work or go to trade elsewhere. They return home to help with the harvest.

Sometimes Malinke migration has proved permanent. The Mali Empire had several trading colonies in West Africa; some are as far away as in Hausa country in modern-day Nigeria. The descendants of those migrant traders, who were (and still are) called *dyula*, still have Malinke settlements there. Malinke first settled in Senegal and Gambia more than 600 years ago, yet Malinke there now still identify themselves as having origins in Mali. More recently, many Malinke travel to parts of Europe and America for business, education, or simply for adventure.

▼ THE ENVIRONMENT ▼

The climate has a rainy season and a dry season. The rainy season begins in May and continues until October. It is a hot time of the year during which rain-bearing monsoon winds blow in from the ocean in the southwest. The rains are vital for agriculture, particularly in those

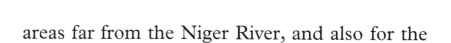

areas far from the Niger River, and also for the herders of small livestock and cattle.

There is more rainfall in the southern parts of Malinke territory than in the north. This influences the type of farm products grown in the two zones. Millet, sorghum, and groundnuts (peanuts) grow better in the north than do such crops as cassava and yam, which require more rainfall.

The first month of the rains is usually a busy period. People try to plant their seeds, particularly rice, in fields that have been previously cleared and tilled in preparation for sowing. After the planting season comes the work of weeding, tending, and harvesting. These farming duties occupy the entire population. Every available hand is needed to gather in the harvest to safety before the birds, other animals, and bad weather can damage it.

The cooler dry season lasts from November until April. From November to March, cold, dry winds blow into this area from the northeast across the Sahara Desert. Some harvesting of the crops planted during the wet season continues during the early part of the dry season. The harvesting of rice, for instance, reaches its peak toward the middle of December. The harvested produce is consumed during the dry season, although the food seldom seems to last until the next harvest. During these difficult months the

Malinke villagers work together to bring in the harvests. Here rice harvesting in the Gambia is accompanied by a drummer playing the *tam tam* or "talking drum."

Malinke turn their thoughts and hopes to the coming season of plenty.

The northern savanna and the Sahel farther north sometimes suffer from drought. This results in massive losses of crops and livestock. These droughts have also been disastrous for the well-being of the population. The most recent drought occurred during the 1980s. Some northern Malinke communities continue to face the threat of famine because the rainfall in these places is unreliable.▲

Griots or *jeli* use traditional musical instruments such as the *kora*, seen here. These instruments are also used in popular music from West Africa, which is now enjoyed by audiences all over the world.

chapter

3

HISTORY

WHAT WE KNOW ABOUT THE HISTORY OF THE
Malinke comes from three main sources. The
first is oral tradition. The Malinke have an ancient system of transmitting their history by
word of mouth from generation to generation
through professional historians and praise singers. These people are known in their language as
jeli and are more popularly known in the West as
griots. Often their accounts are poetic and accompanied by musical instruments, such as
the harplike *kora* and the small *tam tam* or
"talking drum." Traditional songs and instruments have also influenced contemporary musi-
cians from West Africa, whose music is now enjoyed by audiences all over the world.

It is customary for prominent families and
groups to have their own *griot* to recount their
histories. There is no one definitive history of

At a celebration, members of the audience take turns performing dances to music that includes the beat of the *tam tam*. These Malinke are living in the Gambia.

the Malinke before the formation of their empire in the 1200s. This is because *griots* often give contrasting accounts of the same event. *Griots'* versions may be colored by each *griot's* specific interests. *Griots* may not always be able to recall all of the details of their tales. When they tell their stories there is always a large element of improvisation. Nevertheless, taken together, the *griots'* stories give a good idea of Malinke history.

Oral history is the most important source of information on the history of the Malinke. Contemporary historians use these accounts to understand the Malinke and their relationships with their neighbors in the past. The best known *griot* account is the epic of the great Malinke leader Sunjata (also spelled Sundiata). This is a rare example of an oral epic that has been written down in its entirety. The works of the *jeli* Mamoudou Kouyate were set down by D.T. Niane in 1965.

The second source of material on Malinke history is documentary. These are written accounts by early travelers who wrote about what they saw or what they had been told by others. Early Muslim travelers and writers in Arabic include Ibn Battuta, Ibn Khaldun, Ibn Idrisi, al-Bakari, al-'Umari, and Ibn Sa'id.

The most recent source for reconstructing the history of the Malinke is archeological excavation. Archeologists can learn about a people's past activities from the materials found in diggings at specific sites. This technique has been especially useful in the area of Niani, the capital of the Mali Empire.

Despite these sources, our knowledge about the earliest history of the Malinke is limited. Although they had lived on the savanna for a long time, it was not until the 1200s that the Malinke came together to form the core of the empire that was to bear their name.

▼ FORMATION OF THE EMPIRE ▼
Before the 1200s the Malinke who would

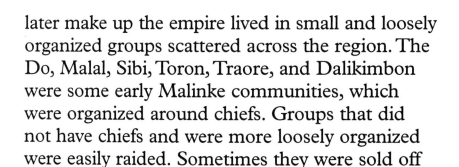

later make up the empire lived in small and loosely organized groups scattered across the region. The Do, Malal, Sibi, Toron, Traore, and Dalikimbon were some early Malinke communities, which were organized around chiefs. Groups that did not have chiefs and were more loosely organized were easily raided. Sometimes they were sold off as slaves to more powerful communities.

One link between these early, separate Malinke communities was that they already spoke similar languages. However, they were not yet strong enough to unite and maintain their independence. These early groups were ruled by the Soninke of the ancient empire of Ghana and later by the Susu (sometimes called Soso). When the Malinke later formed into a large and powerful empire, they joined a long line of rulers of the Sahel and the savanna.

Two major events have shaped the history of the Malinke as we know it today. These events were the introduction of Islam to the western part of West Africa in the eleventh century and the founding of the Mali Empire in the thirteenth century. Although oral histories vary in some details, all mention these two events.

According to oral tradition, the ancestor of the founder of the Mali Empire was Bilali Bounama. He is said to have been an associate of the Prophet Muhammad in Arabia. He had seven sons. His eldest son, Lawalo, left Arabia

At the time of the rise of the Mali Empire in the 1200s, Islam had already been a powerful force in the region for more than 200 years. Seen here is a view of the mosque at Diafarabé in Mali.

and moved to Mali. Lawalo was succeeded by his son Latal Kalabi, who later set up a chiefdom. This chiefdom was extended when it defeated the peoples in the region where Niani was later located. But the chiefdom was not strong enough to compete with its better organized neighbors. The throne was passed on to sons through many generations, until it reached Sunjata, the founder of the Mali Empire.

When Sunjata was born, in the early 1200s, Islam had already existed in the region for more than two hundred years. It had played a crucial role in the fall of the ancient Empire of Ghana in 1076. Because they had been ruled by the Empire of Ghana, the Malinke were also brought under the influence of Islam. Moreover, the various Malinke groups had attracted the attention of the Almoravids—early Muslim raiders who spread Islam to the people they conquered. The oral history of the Malinke from the 1200s onward stresses the connection of the Malinke to Islam so strongly that it distorts earlier Malinke history. The link of Sunjata's ancestor with Arabia is believed to be an example of such Islamic distortion.

After the defeat of the Empire of Ghana by the Almoravids in 1076, Ghana's place as the dominant power in the region was taken by the kingdom of the Susu. Shortly after the birth of

Sunjata the Susu extended their control over the land of the Malinke.

Sunjata began to unite the Malinke chiefdoms under his leadership to liberate his people from Susu domination. Around 1235 Sunjata and his allies defeated the Susu king Sumanguru and founded the Empire of Mali.

After Sunjata's victory, a number of communities that had been under the Susu pledged their loyalty to Sunjata. This was one way in which the empire was extended. The army of the empire marched on, conquering other areas. Minor princes and prominent warriors who had little chance of becoming rulers in their own homes joined Sunjata. They were eager to conquer other lands and establish a rulership there in the name of Sunjata.

Even before this expansion, there had been earlier migrations of Malinke—mainly traders, farmers, and hunters in search of better opportunities. The Malinke moved southwest into Senegal, the Gambia, and toward the coast. These people maintained a strong link with the Malinke heartland while spreading Malinke culture and traditions southward.

The empire also expanded eastward as far as Gao, which later became the capital of the Songhay empire. To the north, the Mali Empire absorbed the lands formerly ruled by the ancient Empire of Ghana and extended its frontiers

Excavations in modern Mali have unearthed many beautiful terracotta sculptures. They were produced between 1100 and 1500 AD, during the period of the Mali Empire and within its boundaries. Experts now believe that they may have been made by a group of Soninke people who were famous warriors and fought for Sunjata and the Mali Empire.

THE "GOLDEN" PILGRIMAGE

Kankan Moussa came to power sometime between 1307 and 1312. He expanded Mali, making it one of the world's largest empires at that time.

Moussa is best known for an epic journey to Egypt and the Middle East in 1324. As a Muslim, Kankan Moussa wanted to make a *hajj*, or pilgrimage, to the holy city of Mecca. Estimates of the size of his entourage vary. He is thought to have taken at least eight thousand followers with him, but some suggest sixty thousand people accompanied him. Even more impressive to those who saw his journey to Egypt and Mecca was the two thousand pounds of gold carried by the Malians.

The emperor's generosity was extraordinary. He made large gifts to the Egyptian ruler and his followers. In fact, he was perhaps too generous. Since he gave so many golden gifts to the Egyptians, the supply of gold in Cairo rose and its price fell. Some sources claim that the gold market in Cairo did not recover for twelve years after the departure of the Malians.

Much like the legend of Sunjata, the story of Kankan Moussa is a source of pride to Malians and to all Africans. That he was received in Arabia and Egypt with respect and awe makes him an even more important symbol of African greatness. In a world where wealth and power were measures of status, Kankan Moussa proved to the world that his African empire was second to none. He also encouraged and supported scholarship and brought back from his pilgrimage an Arab architect who designed magnificent mosques that were centers of Muslim learning.

beyond Timbuktu. The growth of the Mali Empire to the south gave the Malinke direct access to the gold mines of the forest regions of Bure and Bambuk. Though most Malinke were farmers, gold was crucial in trans-Saharan trade. Gold also helped the Malinke maintain diplomatic links with Egypt, Arabia, and Morocco. The control of gold supply and trade in the region was the key to power.

Kankan Moussa, the famous Emperor of Mali, brought back an architect from his pilgrimage to Arabia to design beautiful new mosques. Mosques in cities like Timbuktu, Jenne, and Gao were important centers of learning that became famous throughout the Muslim world. Seen here is the beautiful mosque at Jenne (top), and a smaller mosque in Sokoroba in Côte d'Ivoire.

The Malinke Empire peaked in power around 1350. Thereafter, many problems contributed to its decline. First, there were frequent quarrels within the ruling family about who should succeed to the throne. Sometimes these quarrels led to violence and conspiracies that weakened the rulership. Taking advantage of these weaknesses, some groups under Malinke control stood up for their freedom.

As the empire expanded, its size made it difficult to control all the areas effectively from the center. Those on the edges of Malinke territory began to assert their independence, like the Tuaregs in the mid-1300s. At about the same time neighboring peoples such as the Songhay, the Mossi, and the Bamana began to seize parts of the Mali Empire and make them part of their own states.

As the Mali Empire declined, the Malinke dispersed to many places in their region of West Africa. This encouraged intermarriage and the mixture of populations, especially in the southern parts of West Africa. The mixture of peoples in this part of Africa made it easier for people to move around and trade. It also built and promoted the ties between different cultures.

Though the western parts of the Mali Empire in Senegal and the Gambia remained strong, the decline of the Empire in other areas was so great that it effected these strong areas as well. By the

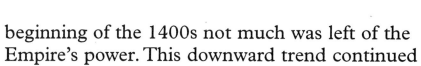

beginning of the 1400s not much was left of the Empire's power. This downward trend continued until, by the end of the 1600s, the descendants of Sunjata held only the small state of Kangaba.

A number of kingdoms followed the Mali Empire. The kingdoms were frequently ruled by a *faama*, a warlord, who may or may not have been born in the region he conquered. These were conqueror kings; sometimes they were Muslim and used the conquest of "infidels" as an excuse to lead wars of conquest.

The Empire of Mali was no longer a force to reckon with in the 1600s and 1700s when West Africa's trade with the Euro-American world was at its height. The Malinke were unable to prevent the takeover of their land by Europeans in the coming centuries.

▼ COLONIALISM ▼

The colonists' main goal in the Malinke areas of West Africa was to make profits trading gold, slaves, and cash crops.

By the end of the 1700s the transatlantic slave trade had slowed. This was a devastating blow to the Malinke rulers, who had gained much of their wealth by taxing slave traders who crossed their land. It was a great relief to Malinke farmers who had been terrorized by slavery and suffered severe disruptions in their way of life.

When the western savanna was colonized,

only local kings, warlords, and chiefs were left to deal with the French, British, and Portuguese. These leaders had little power, however, since the Mali Empire had fallen by then. It had been absorbed by the Songhai empire, which fell to Moroccan armies in 1591.

The colonists further reduced the kings' power by putting them on a fixed salary. The colonists also eliminated the kings' primary means of control and wealth, which was their ability to tax and fine their subjects and passing traders. The French colonized the largest numbers of Malinke: Guinea, Senegal, Côte d'Ivoire, and Mali are all ex-French colonies.

The Malinke were known as fine traders. The colonists saw the advantage of allowing them to continue trading. It was important to the Europeans, however, that this profitable trade now be run to benefit them. To achieve this, they hired loyal Africans to take over the leadership of Malinke villages on the colonists' behalf.

In the 1800s the colonists put great pressure on Malinke rulers, the *mansas*, to be passive as they lost control of their villages. The Malinke were threatened both with violence and economic sanctions if they did not give in to European demands. This was not acceptable to the Malinke, who resisted this outrage as fiercely as they could. However, they rarely had access to modern weapons. Besides, they were now more

At Independence Day celebrations in Banjul, capital city of the Gambia, a policeman keeps a watchful eye on the crowd. Malinke are integrated in the populations of the many multiethnic countries in West Africa where they live.

than ever economically dependent on the French; to anger them was to invite starvation.

During the twentieth century a spirit of independence awakened in Africa. The colonists were rejected and new self-governing republics formed. By the early 1960s the independence of Senegal, Guinea, Mali, Côte d'Ivoire, and the Gambia had been declared.▲

chapter

4

TRADITIONS AND CUSTOMS

AMONG THE MALINKE, STATUS IN SOCIETY IS determined through one's father's family. The Malinke's first loyalty is to their families. The concept of family includes a much larger group than what Europeans and Americans may understand by that word. It often includes a man, who is head of the family, his wife (more often wives) and children, the wives and children of his sons, and his unmarried daughters. His brothers and their children could also be members of this family. Several such large family units are brought together to form villages. These villages, in turn, make up larger territories.

An important aspect of the traditions and customs of the Malinke is polygyny. This means that Malinke men can have more than one wife at a time. Such marriages are encouraged both by Malinke tradition and the teachings and

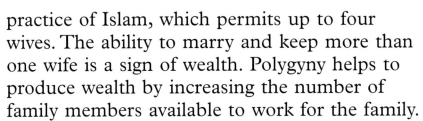

practice of Islam, which permits up to four wives. The ability to marry and keep more than one wife is a sign of wealth. Polygyny helps to produce wealth by increasing the number of family members available to work for the family.

In the rural setting each wife is provided with her own house within the family's compound. A traditional Malinke house is round. These homes are made of mud brick known as "banco"— similar to adobe—and have cone-shaped thatched roofs. Today they are often made of cement blocks roofed with corrugated metal sheets. A woman lives with her children in her own house. The compound is surrounded by a wall so that the entire family of related men, their wives, and their children are marked as a single unit.

It is not customary for a man to approach a woman he would like to marry. Rather, he takes a friend or two and visits the father of the woman to make his request. The suitor brings kola nuts to his prospective in-laws. If the parents are favorably disposed to the request, they accept the kola nuts. They then state what valuables the suitor is expected to give to his new wife's family. This is called the bridewealth. It compensates the family of the woman, which, by marrying out its daughter, has lost a member of the family labor force.

Agreeing to the bridewealth shows that the

The Malinke now live throughout the world and in many different kinds of homes. These homes in Mali show traditional architecture (top), which has changed little over the centuries, and a village street where the buildings are more Westernized (bottom). Many Malinke women are still responsible for the collection of firewood (top) and the distribution of food (bottom).

groom's proposal is serious. Through the bride-wealth the two families become linked economically as well as socially. It is expected that the groom will need some time—even several years after the wedding—to pay all that he owes. That payment period is a time to strengthen the bond between the families.

▼ SOCIAL HIERARCHY ▼

Traditionally, Malinke society is divided into several groups, each with different rights, privileges, and obligations. These groups form an order of social rank, called a hierarchy. At the top of the hierarchy are the members of the royal lineages, usually the founders of the community. They have the greatest privileges and are highly respected by other members of the society. In the past, members of this group were very wealthy because they could demand and use the labor of the less privileged groups on their farms. Slave raids among more helpless peoples was another method through which the royalty acquired wealth. They also had taxes and tributes paid to them.

A small group of Islamic experts and teachers occupy a place below the royalty. The royal advisers are traditionally chosen from this group. This has been the case since the time of the Mali Empire, when these experts and teachers were the only people who could read and write

Families of specialized artisans may become very wealthy through the use of their skills, but they have low social status in Malinke society. Here the women of the Bamba family, who live in Odienné in Côte d'Ivoire, are seen making pottery.

in Arabic. They were at that time the administrators, secretaries, and managers of the empire's finances. They also controlled the knowledge of how to prepare the charms, talismans, and potions that had spiritual power.

The next social level is the commoners. During the reign of the Mali Empire, soldiers were drawn from this class. The state's agriculture also depended on the commoners. Commoners received little reward for their important contributions to society, however. They were often taxed by the nobility, who also demanded their products.

Below the commoners were several classes of specialized artisans, including potters, leatherworkers, blacksmiths and *griots*. *Griots* were "wordsmiths"—anything to do with words and songs was their speciality. Their task was to record and relate history and to entertain. Artisans could become very rich on account of their skills and because they provided necessary services. But they had, and continue to have, low social status. Their professions are usually passed down from one generation to the next. They are rarely allowed to marry outside their group.

The final group to mention is the slaves. The societies of the savanna were noted for their slave raids and slave markets. As one state succeeded another in this area, captives were often products of the conflicts. Many of these captives were sold in the local slave markets; others were transported to lands far away. Even when there was peace between the major states, there was no guarantee that more helpless peoples would not be raided. Privileged people were able to acquire slaves as a result of these activities.

As individuals, slaves could achieve a high position in their master's household. In theory, slaves could buy their freedom, but this was very difficult to do. It is only within the last hundred years that slavery has become illegal in these areas. Even now its effects are still felt by the descendants of former slaves.

This traditional hierarchy still exists in Malinke society. However, the royalty no longer

The men of the Bamba family are specialist blacksmiths.

have power beyond their surrounding villages. Their roles are symbolic reminders of the strong empire of centuries ago. Modern government has now taken over the powers that kings once held. Literacy is now widespread in urban areas. As a result, more people have an opportunity to participate in government or prosper in business.

▼ MALINKE RELIGION ▼

The traditional Malinke belief system centers around a number of deities and spirits connected to the local environment. These beings are believed to be in direct contact with the people and to influence their welfare. They cause the population to multiply and provide abundant harvests. The people appeal to their power to do good or prevent evil through prayer and sacrifices. In pre-Islamic times, the rulers (*mansa*) of Malinke communities were regarded as having both spiritual and secular powers. Help was obtained from the deities and the spirits of the ancestors through the *mansa*.

These ancient religious ideas determined the people's view of the world and the powers that controlled it. After the introduction of Islam, the world of the Malinke continued to be affected by the *jinn* (magical beings that can appear in human forms) and other spiritual influences. Even today it is common for people beginning a journey or project to strengthen and protect themselves with *gri gri* (charms and talismans). The mixture of traditional beliefs and practices with Islamic faith has remained an important mark of Malinke religious life.

The lifestyle changes brought by Islam were enormous. Changes in behavior were expected

Dramane Coulibaly, from Nienesso in Côte d'Ivoire, wears many *gri gri* in his role as the praise singer of hunters, who need charms to protect them against the many dangers they face.

to occur upon conversion. Those who believed in Islam did not drink alcohol or eat pork. The meat they did eat had to be slaughtered according to strict rules. The observed long periods of fasting. Every believer was expected to be able to read the holy Koran. Every Muslim was expected to make a pilgrimage to Mecca during his or her lifetime, an enormous responsibility for people in those days of travel by horse, camel, and wooden ship.

Islam changed the structure of society as well. These changes did not come all at once, but became common practice over centuries of influence. The *mansas* and their advisers found their authority questioned. Traditional Malinke laws were no longer sufficient because now the religious principles of Islam were the higher power. Initiated age grades in the villages found themselves with the new responsibility of looking after the place used many times a day for prayer to Allah.

Today, these tenets of Islam are followed in various degrees by Malinke who consider themselves Muslim. Still, aspects of traditional Malinke religion are always present.▲

chapter

5

DAILY LIFE

EVEN AT THE HEIGHT OF THE MALI EMPIRE
the village was the hub of traditional life for most
Malinke. Malinke villages were divided into
wards, which were in turn subdivided into quarters. Each village was ruled by the descendants
of those who founded it. The head of the village
was usually the eldest man among the eligible
class. The village government was made up of
the ruler, heads of the wards and the quarters,
and the heads of the families. It was essentially a
government by elders. In this traditional context
the elders are still considered the most experi-
enced people in the population. Together they
embody the collective wisdom as handed down
by the forefathers of the community.

A major function of traditional village government was to act as a peacekeeping body. The
guiding principle in settling village disputes was

to promote reconciliation, thus restoring harmony in the village. There was hardly any alternative to this line of action. After all, a village was not large enough for groups to avoid each other all the time.

Malinke villages still exist in the traditional form in rural areas. Each village is made up of several families. Each family is an economic unit, producing most of what it eats. It holds several pieces of farmland of various sizes. Some of this is kept as land for the benefit of the whole family. The eldest male family member, usually the head of the household, controls this land on behalf of all the members. Aside from this, some plots of land are given to certain members of the family individually. Among the Malinke, female members of the family may have their own plots or farms.

During the farming season, all able-bodied family members are expected to farm with the head of the family. It is important for everyone to work on the general land, both to contribute to the well-being of the family and to show respect for the head of the household. Toward the end of the afternoon individual members may work on their own farms. Sometimes the pattern is varied to enable members to work together for five days, thus allowing the rest of the week for their private farms.

Certain tasks are assigned specifically to men,

Malinke villages built in the traditional way still exist in Mali. Here can be seen the seating platform for elders and the specially designed window that allows the free flow of air through the house.

These newly circumcised boys in the Gambia are presented to the public at the celebration dances held after circumcision.

to women, or to children. Men clear the undergrowth and prepare the land for the farming season. They plant and manage particular crops, like millet and sorghum, that are identified with men. In addition, men are responsible for hunting, herding, leatherwork, smithing, warfare, and the building of houses.

Young boys are taught to take care of men's crops and to herd cattle. They scare off birds and small rodents from the farms. At an appropriate time in their lives all boys are initiated into the responsibilities of manhood. This is the period when the young men are circumcised. Children of a similar age undergo circumcision at the same time, whether their parents are royals or commoners. Those who go through an initiation together feel a bond with each other that lasts a lifetime.

The bulk of women's activities is in the household. Children are mainly cared for by their mother, who is often assisted by the other female family members. Young children are given a lot of liberty to play and explore their surroundings under the watchful eyes of their mothers and siblings. Women are also traders and artisans. While only men weave, today many women sew with sewing machines and continue to spin thread as they did in the past.

Children grow up with the strong impression that their mothers are devoted to them. Mothers not only serve as the protectors of their children, but also contribute to their education at home. Mothers recite folk stories and legends to their children at night. This is an important channel through which Malinke customs are transmitted. As if to repay their mothers for all their kindness, love, and care, Malinke children generally hold their mothers in very high regard.

In addition to their household responsibilities, women also work on their farm, usually near the home. They are responsible for the provision of daily food staples. Rice, for example, is traditionally a women's crop.

During the farming season one or two women stay at home and prepare the food for the workers. When it is ready the food is taken to the

Girls and young women are trained to pound the grains eaten by the Malinke. Today there are many Western-educated Malinke women working in cities in the countries where the Malinke live.

farm. Men eat separately from the women. The most common food is boiled millet flour mixed with milk. A more special fare consists of rice with meat and peanut sauce. If the farm is very far from home the things needed for lunch might be taken to the farm and cooked there.

From an early age girls are encouraged to learn the role of women both at home and on the farm. They learn how to pound grains and are taught the process of turning the flour into food. They also learn how to spin cotton, fetch firewood, and draw water. Likewise, young boys learn their roles by watching their fathers and older brothers.

Malinke women play "water drums" made from gourds filled with water. These drummers are from the Gambia.

In rural areas, learning from oral tradition and following role models are still the most common types of education among the Malinke. Traditional education begins at birth and continues throughout a person's life. In urban centers Malinke youth are likely to attend Islamic or Western style schools.

Urban life for Malinke varies according to where they live in West Africa or the world.▲

Although most Malinke are Muslim, many aspects of pre-Islamic Malinke religion are blended into their practice of Islam. Here a sand reader from Côte d'Ivoire foretells future good and bad luck from marks made in the sand. He tries to block bad luck by pressing kola nuts into the bad marks.

6

A VIEW OF THE FUTURE

THE MALINKE MADE OUTSTANDING CONTRIB-
utions to the development of the western savanna. The Mali Empire was much larger than any
previous state in the area. As military men,
hunters, farmers, and traders, the Malinke
themselves were mostly responsible for expanding this empire. Expansion and settlement
brought prosperity to the Malinke and spread
their culture.

Before and during the empire, long-term
Malinke settlements were occupied in the name
of their ruler (*mansa*) back in Mali. Even today,
Malinke throughout Africa and the world still
regard their original home in Mali as the au-
thentic source of their culture. Visits to their
Malian home base are encouraged. The *griots*
who travel through widely scattered Malinke
communities reinforce traditional beliefs, history,

customs, and language. In fact, the Malinke language has gained much strength in the past few decades. In the Gambia, for instance, when peoples of diverse cultures gather they are likely to conduct their discussions in Malinke.

The strong cultural link among the scattered Malinke served as a unifying bond. This bond gave them a forceful voice in the political movement against colonialism in the early 1960s. The Malinke have retained this advantage in countries where they are well represented in the government. Since independence, several heads of state in West Africa have been of Malinke origin.

An important advantage of the shared language and outlook among the Malinke is that it has enabled them to maintain strong links between each other despite being widely scattered. With this guaranteed and expanding trade link, the economic future of the Malinke seems assured, even though competition is increasing on all sides.

Shrewd business people, the Malinke have learned to adapt quickly to changing conditions. From early on they were traders in agricultural products and livestock. They took a major part in the slave trade. When the gold mines came under their control they succeeded in that trade as well. In the twentieth century they have turned to the production of cash crops for

Today the Malinke live among people of many different cultures. This Gambian courtyard is shared by people of Malinke, Wolof, and Serer backgrounds.

profit. Their rich experience in business and their proven ability to adapt to changing market conditions prepare them to face the future with confidence.

While cultural connections help urban merchants, rural villages experience different pressures. Though traditionally there was some surplus food for sale, most of the produce was for the use of the family. With the increasing importance of rice and groundnuts as cash crops, changes are now taking place. For example, women have traditionally been associated with staple crops. The change to cash crops has brought about a change in attitude toward these

Malinke men and women throughout West Africa are involved in projects
to develop their countries for everyone's benefit. Here they participate
in a soybean project using the latest farming methods.

traditions. As a result, women's claim to land
ownership is being questioned. The emphasis on
cash crops also reduces the availability of food in
the village. Although most rural Malinke live in
the savanna, they have recently suffered from
food scarcity. These agricultural changes are
causes for concern about the future.

However, the urban and commercial aspects
of Malinke society are thriving. In addition to
their long-standing trade skills, the Malinke
have found other ways to advance themselves.
For example, they have embraced Western
education, which prepares young Malinke for
careers in the world market.

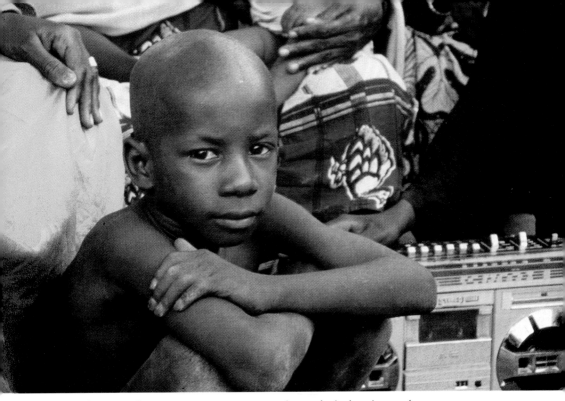

This *griot* boy is using a tape recorder to help him learn the many songs, stories, and histories that make up the rich Malinke tradition. Whatever the future may hold, it seems that Malinke tradition and the great achievements of the Mali Empire will not be forgotten.

▼ CONCLUSION ▼

Islam took root among the Malinke about a thousand years ago. The Malinke's association with a thriving world religion promotes their acceptance in West Africa. It is also helpful in forming and sustaining business contacts. Their moderate view of Islam may be the best path toward peaceful relationships in West Africa, where many communities still adhere to their ancestors' religions. The Malinke have learned that religious tolerance and moderation promote peace and productivity. When the Empire took over the gold-producing regions of Bure and Bambuk, efforts to convert the local miners to

MALINKE PROVERBS

kuno se lii, naanaa mee lii.
Your hair can be styled as you please; your future cannot.

maxafeno le se kinoo diyaa.
The sauce makes the dish delicious.

kanijuo man kunan bari a dino ye kunan.
The spice plant is not pungent, but its shoots are.
(Sons are not always like their father.)

suo se i bori, i se a lafaa busa la.
You can make a horse gallop faster with the help of a whip.
(Some people need extra encouragement to give their all.)

moxo mee i buloo bula saanaa to.
A person shouldn't put his hands in snake's poison.
(There is no point in taking a risk that gains nothing).

kuma se mee daa fula le to.
In two mouths conversation lives long. (It is easy to maintain a friendship when both people give and trust equally.)

Islam resulted in the workers running away. This event showed the benefits of maintaining religious tolerance.

The Malinke have a bright future in West Africa, and the heritage of the Empire of Mali will always be remembered.▲

Glossary

age grades Group of people of the same age.

Almoravids A political and religious group from North Africa who spread Islam to parts of West Africa through the use of force.

arafang Designated teacher of a young child.

dyula Migrant traders.

gri gri Charms and talismans meant to aid people in various activities.

griots (in Malinke, *jeli*) Traditional oral historians and praise singers.

harmattan Cold, dry northeast wind that blows into West Africa during the dry season from across the Sahara Desert.

jinn Magical being with mysterious power and capable of appearing in human forms.

kora Malinke traditional harp with twenty-one strings, used for social occasions.

mansa Malinke traditional name for their rulers.

polygyny A type of marriage in which a man marries more than one wife. It is popularly called polygamy.

tam tam A small drum used by the *griot* during public ceremonies.

For Further Reading

Bovill, E. W. *The Golden Trade*. Oxford: Oxford
University Press, 1968.
Chu, D., and Skinner, E. *Glorious Age in Africa:
The Story of Three Great African Empires.*
Trenton, NJ: Africa World Press, 1965.
Levtzion, N. *Ancient Ghana and Mali*. London:
Methuen, 1973.
Rosenthal, Ricky. *The Splendor That Was Africa*.
New York: Oceanic Publications Inc., 1967.
Wisniewski, David. *Sundiata: Lion King of Mali*.
New York: Clarion, 1992.

CHALLENGING READING

Gaily, Harry A., Jr. *A History of the Gambia*.
London: Routledge & Kegan Paul, 1964.
Niane, D. T. *Sundiata: An Epic of Old Mali*.
London: Longman, Green and Co., 1965.
Quinn, Charlotte A. *Mandingo Kingdoms of the
Senegambia*. Evanston, IL: Northwestern
University Press, 1972.
Sonko-Godwin, Patience. *Ethnic Groups of the
Senegambia: A Brief History*. Gambia: Sunrise
Publishers Ltd., 1985.

Index

ABOUT THE AUTHOR
C. Onyeka Nwanunobi holds a B.A. with honors in History from the University of Nigeria, Nsukka, and an M.A. and a Ph.D. from the University of Toronto. He has taught at both places and is presently in the Department of Anthropology at the University of Toronto. He has published in Africa, Europe, and North America.

CONSULTING EDITOR: Gary N. van Wyk, Ph.D.

ACKNOWLEDGEMENTS: The publishers gratefully acknowledge the kind assistance given to this volume by the Malinke scholars Dr. Barbara Hoffman and Dr. Jeanne Maddox Toungara.

PHOTO CREDITS: Cover, pp. 8, 12, 20, 37 top, 37 bottom, 49, 59 © Barbara Hoffman, Ph.D.; pp. 14, 16, 30 bottom, 39, 41, 43, 54, 58 © Jeanne Maddox Toungara, Ph.D.; pp. 15, 25, 30 top © Chris Caldicott; pp. 19, 22, 34, 44, 45, 50, 52, 53, 57 © Robert L. Thompson; p. 28 © Roger Asselbergh, Brussels, courtesy of Bernard De Grunne.

LAYOUT AND DESIGN: Kim Sonsky